**45 SWEET AND SAVORY RECIPES** for Shortcakes, Hand Pies, Salad, Salsas, and More

# Strawberry Love

### Cynthia Graubart

Storey Publishing

*To Norman and Rachel*
*You add the sweetness to my life*

*The mission of Storey Publishing is to serve our customers by*
*publishing practical information that encourages*
*personal independence in harmony with the environment.*

Edited by Deanna F. Cook and Sarah Guare
Art direction and book design by Alethea Morrison
Text production by Liseann Karandisecky
Indexed by Christine R. Lindemer, Boston Road Communications
Cover and interior photography by © Keller + Keller Photography
Author photo (back cover flap) by Just Bartee Photography
Food and prop styling by Catrine Kelty

Storey books are available at special discounts
when purchased in bulk for premiums and
sales promotions as well as for fund-raising or
educational use. Special editions or book excerpts
can also be created to specification. For details,
please call 800-827-8673, or send an email to
sales@storey.com.

**Storey Publishing**
210 MASS MoCA Way
North Adams, MA 01247
*storey.com*

Printed in China through World Print
10 9 8 7 6 5 4 3 2 1

Library of Congress Cataloging-in-Publication Data
on file

# Contents

# SWEET SCARLET BERRIES

When fresh strawberry season arrives, I lock in a date to visit my local U-pick farm to stock up on the plump ruby gems, filling my back seat with quart after quart of the heavenly scented fruit. A glorious time in my kitchen awaits, turning my field-ripened harvest into savory and sweet jams, thick syrups and shrubs, and desserts of every kind holding aloft the scarlet berries in clouds of billowy whipped cream.

Strawberries are native to North America, and today's cultivated varieties are descendants of a strawberry variety from Virginia crossed with a Chilean variety. Every US state grows strawberries, but California cultivates roughly 90 percent of the commercial crop (about 34,000 acres), with Florida in second place, producing about 8 percent (about 10,700 acres), including all of the winter crop. A single acre of strawberries can produce as much as 50,000 pounds of fruit in a single season. Each field is picked multiple times, as the berries ripen in stages.

Strawberry plants are low to the ground. During their natural growing season, a little white berry emerges from a white flower and grows into a luscious, red, heart-shaped bulb. You may be surprised to learn that strawberries are a member of the rose family and aren't even classified as a berry at all. Botanically speaking, they are an aggregate of achenes — those little black seeds (the true fruits) that form on the outside of the receptacle (the fleshy, edible part we enjoy).

Ancient Romans used wild strawberries to treat everything from fever to sore throats and even depression. Native Americans used strawberries to treat sores and steeped leaves and roots into teas that treated gum and internal inflammations. Today we know that the fruit is high in vitamin C — one serving has more vitamin C than an orange — and is a great source of folate and potassium, all of which contribute to bone strength and lower blood pressure. Research suggests that the flavonoids responsible for the red color in strawberries (and the blue in blueberries) have antioxidant and

anti-inflammatory properties and may improve heart health, help manage diabetes, support brain health, mediate inflammation, and reduce the risk of some cancers. It's no wonder strawberries are considered a superfruit!

The recipes that follow feature strawberries at their best for any time of day. Savory recipes bring out the more complex flavors of the fruit, while the sweet recipes make for easy breakfasts and snacks and showstopping desserts. So whether it's Strawberry Gazpacho (page 26) or Pork Chops with Strawberry-Balsamic Sauce (page 34), Strawberry Crumb Cake (page 7) or Pink Strawberry Pie with Lattice Crust (page 56), there's a recipe here for every taste and occasion.

## Tips for Cooking with Strawberries

**When purchasing fresh strawberries,** choose berries that are firm, plump, fully red, and free from moisture. Organic berries, where available, are pesticide-free and are a healthier choice.

**Pick strawberries in the morning,** when the fruit is still cool, as the heat of the day makes the berries more fragile. Local U-pick farms are a fun outing for the whole family. To pick a strawberry, hold the stem between your forefinger and thumbnail about 1 inch above the fruit, resting the strawberry in your palm. Pinch the stem to break it apart and release the berry, then move it to a shallow container. Avoid filling a container more than 3 inches deep, to reduce the chance of the berries being crushed.

**Strawberries should be stored** unwashed and refrigerated, and only washed immediately before use. Fresh berries keep refrigerated just a few days, so use them up quickly or freeze.

**To hull strawberries,** use the tip of a small knife to score around the edge of the stem end of the berry and lift out the leafy top and hard core underneath. Another method uses a straw inserted into the bottom end of the strawberry up through the stem end. The core and leafy top are trapped in the top end of the straw. Pinch the straw and draw it out of the strawberry to remove the core.

**To slice strawberries,** place them hulled-side down and slice vertically.

**Frozen strawberries** are widely available in 3-pound bags, making them ideal for keeping on hand year-round.

**To freeze fresh strawberries,** slice off the top, place the berries cut-side down on a parchment paper–lined baking sheet, and freeze. When frozen solid, move to freezer bags.

**You can substitute frozen strawberries for fresh** in recipes where the strawberry is fully cooked, or fully incorporated into a mixture that is whirred in a food processor or blender. Most recipes will note if the berries should be used frozen, or thawed before using.

**To boost strawberry flavor** in a recipe, add some freeze-dried strawberries that have been pulverized into a powder.

**Strawberries are easily substituted** for other summer fruit in your favorite recipes for cobblers, crisps, and most other sweet treats.

**To dry your own strawberries,** wash and hull the strawberries. Cut the berries in half except if they are large: Cut those in quarters. Spread out the cut berries in a single layer on a parchment-lined baking sheet and place in a preheated 200°F (95°C) oven. Rotate the pan every 30 to 45 minutes, drying for about 3 hours. Remove the baking sheet and allow to cool for 30 minutes. Check a thick strawberry by breaking it in half. If any moisture is detected, return the pan to the oven for 30 minutes. Transfer the dried berries to a ziplock bag or plastic container and store in an area away from sunlight. Watch for signs of condensation, which can encourage mold. If it occurs, redry the berries for another hour or so.

# Cook's Notes

### INGREDIENTS
Quality ingredients yield quality results, so purchase the best-quality ingredients your food budget allows. Several baking recipes call for certain ingredients to be at room temperature. This provides for the best texture in cakes and muffins, and it also allows for some ingredients to be more easily integrated with others.

**Baking powder and soda.** Fresh baking powder and baking soda (less than 1 year old) are essential to baking success.

**Butter.** Unless otherwise specified, the butter used in these recipes may be unsalted or salted.

**Cream and milk.** Heavy whipping cream is cream with at least 36 percent butterfat and is the best choice for rich, thick, billowy tufts of cream to be folded into dessert recipes or dolloped atop individual servings. Recipes calling for whole milk are best made with whole milk. Recipes not specifying can be made with any milk on hand.

**Eggs.** Large eggs are the standard for these recipes.

**Freeze-dried strawberries.** Pack a punch of strawberry flavor into a recipe by adding freeze-dried strawberries. Sold in many grocery and specialty foods stores around the country, a bag weighing 1.2 ounces is made from 12 ounces of ripe strawberries freeze-dried at the peak of freshness. Not only are they useful for adding taste to less-than-perfect fresh strawberries, they also improve the color, making dishes using paler strawberries appear more robust. Recipes here call for blitzing the freeze-dried strawberries into a powder using a food processor or blender.

**Lemon juice.** Freshly squeezed lemon juice is preferred in recipes where the juice isn't heated during cooking, or in recipes where lemon is a dominant flavor.

**Self-rising flour.** For recipes calling for self-rising flour, you may substitute 1 cup all-purpose flour mixed with 1½ teaspoons baking powder and ¼ teaspoon salt. Flour is best stored in an airtight container and can remain fresh for up to 1 year if stored this way in a dry cabinet. Storing flour in the freezer extends the freshness up to 2 years.

**Spices.** For maximum flavor, restock spices that are more than 1 year old.

**Vanilla extract.** Use pure or imitation as your preference dictates. A well-respected food magazine conducted a blind taste test in which the participants preferred imitation vanilla for its simple vanilla taste. Suit your own taste buds.

## METHODS

Whisk dry ingredients together for at least 30 seconds to encourage the full incorporation of all of the dry ingredients. This is essential when making recipes that include baking powder, baking soda, or salt.

To measure flour by the cup, lightly whisk the flour in its container, then spoon the flour into a dry measure and level it off with the back of a knife. If you are using a scale, 120 grams of flour equals 1 cup.

## EQUIPMENT

**Baking pans.** Glass pie pans produce the crispiest crusts. Follow the visual cues for doneness as you get to know any new equipment.

**Oven.** Temperatures vary widely among ovens, and ovens often have hot spots. To identify hot spots in your oven, line a baking sheet with slices of store-bought white bread and bake the slices at 350°F (180°C). As the bread is toasting, you'll be able to identify the oven's hot spots by noticing which slices brown more quickly. Purchase an oven thermometer, an inexpensive insurance policy, to know how far off your oven temperature may be and compensate accordingly. You can also improve results for most baked goods by turning them 180 degrees from front to back halfway through the baking time.

**Instant-read thermometer.** Use this kitchen essential to determine if ingredients have been cooked to a proper temperature under food safety guidelines. It's another inexpensive tool to enhance your cooking.

**Electric hand mixer.** The time cues in the recipes that follow are written with these mixers in mind. If you are using a stand mixer, use the whisk attachment for egg whites and whipping cream, and the paddle attachment for all other ingredients. Watch for the visual cues for doneness as described in the recipes, knowing that a stand mixer will produce results more quickly than a hand mixer.

# Strawberry Crumb Cake

## *(a.k.a. Coffee Cake)*

**MAKES ONE 9-INCH
SQUARE CAKE**

## Topping

- ¾ cup all-purpose flour
- ⅓ cup granulated sugar
- ⅓ cup firmly packed light brown sugar
- 1 teaspoon ground cinnamon
- Pinch of ground nutmeg
- Pinch of salt
- ⅓ cup unsalted butter, melted

## Cake

- ⅓ cup butter, at room temperature
- ⅔ cup granulated sugar
- 2 eggs, at room temperature
- 1 teaspoon vanilla extract
- 1½ cups all-purpose flour
- 1 tablespoon baking powder
- ½ teaspoon salt
- ⅔ cup milk, at room temperature
- 1 cup fresh strawberries, hulled and chopped

*This crumb cake is lovely for a morning coffee break, but it is truly wonderful any time of day. The crumb topping is ample — just like in the big bakeries. Room-temperature ingredients contribute to the light texture of the cake.*

### MAKE THE TOPPING

1. Whisk together the flour, sugars, cinnamon, nutmeg, and salt in a small bowl until thoroughly combined, at least 30 seconds. Pour the melted butter over the flour mixture and work the butter into the mixture using your fingers or a fork until completely mixed. Set aside.

### MAKE THE CAKE

2. Preheat the oven to 375°F (190°C). Spray or grease and flour a 9-inch square baking pan.

3. Beat the butter and sugar together in a large bowl with an electric hand mixer until light in color and fluffy, about 4 minutes. Beat in the eggs and vanilla until combined.

4. Whisk together the flour, baking powder, and salt in a medium bowl until thoroughly combined, at least 30 seconds. Add the dry ingredients to the butter mixture in thirds, alternating with half the milk, beating until combined and scraping the bottom between each addition. Gently fold in the strawberries.

5. Transfer the batter to the prepared pan, leveling with a spatula, and sprinkle evenly with the crumble topping. Bake for 35 to 40 minutes, or until a toothpick inserted in the center comes out clean (avoiding a strawberry). Cool for 10 minutes in the pan before cutting into squares. Serve warm.

# Puff Pastry Braided Strawberry Danish

**MAKES 4–6 SERVINGS**

- 4 ounces mascarpone or cream cheese, at room temperature

- 1 sheet frozen puff pastry, thawed

- 5 large or 7 medium fresh strawberries, hulled and sliced

- 1 egg

- 1 tablespoon water

  Decorating sugar or other large-grain sugar

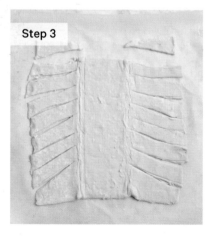

Step 3

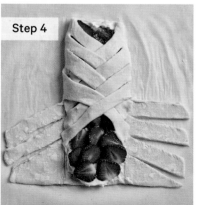

Step 4

*Homemade breakfast pastries are so easy to make using frozen puff pastry. This braided Danish is gorgeous, with its overlapping strips of dough creating an eye-catching faux braid.*

1. Preheat the oven to 400°F (200°C). Line a baking sheet with parchment paper.

2. Stir the mascarpone in a small bowl until smooth and spreadable.

3. Flatten the puff pastry on the prepared baking sheet. Score the dough with the tip of a small sharp knife to make three long rectangles — just barely marking the dough, not cutting through. Make diagonal slits in the dough on each of the side rectangles, about 1 inch apart, cutting all the way through. Cut away the top corners from the upper left and right of the dough. (See photo at left.)

4. Spread the mascarpone down the center third of the dough using an offset spatula. Top with overlapping layers of strawberry slices. Fold the strips of pastry over the center, crisscrossing over the filling and alternating strips from one side to the other (see photo at left). Fold down the bottom flap of dough and pinch to seal.

5. Whisk the egg and water together in a small bowl. Brush the egg wash over the entire Danish and sprinkle with decorating sugar.

6. Bake for 25 to 30 minutes, or until puffed and golden brown.

7. Transfer to a wire rack to cool before slicing.

# Strawberry-Orange Muffins

**MAKES 12 MUFFINS**

Zest of 1 orange

1 cup sugar

3 cups all-purpose flour

4 teaspoons baking powder

½ teaspoon salt

½ teaspoon ground cinnamon

1 cup milk

2 eggs

1 teaspoon vanilla extract

½ cup canola or other neutral oil

1½ cups fresh strawberries, hulled and roughly chopped

*Citrus and strawberries are a complementary pair. These muffins straddle the line between breakfast and snack perfectly. You choose.*

1. Preheat the oven to 375°F (190°C). Line a 12-cup muffin pan with paper cup liners, or spray with cooking spray and set aside.

2. Place the orange zest and sugar in a medium bowl. Using your fingers, rub until thoroughly combined. Add in the flour, baking powder, salt, and cinnamon, and whisk until completely incorporated, at least 30 seconds.

3. Whisk together the milk, eggs, vanilla, and oil in a large bowl. Stir in the flour mixture until just combined. Gently fold in the berries. Spoon the batter into the prepared muffin cups.

4. Bake for about 25 minutes, until the tops are lightly golden and a toothpick inserted in the center comes out clean (avoiding a strawberry). Turn the muffins out onto a wire rack. Serve warm, or cool completely and store refrigerated.

# Homemade Strawberry Butter

**MAKES 1½ CUPS**

1 cup (2 sticks) unsalted butter, at room temperature

3 tablespoons water

½ teaspoon salt

½ cup fresh strawberries, hulled and smashed

¼ cup confectioners' sugar, plus more as needed

*Strawberry butter is an indulgent spread for toasted bread of any kind, or slathered inside a warm muffin, or melted atop homemade pancakes or waffles. Whichever you choose, it will be a welcome treat.*

1. Beat the butter, water, and salt in a deep mixing bowl with an electric hand mixer until fluffy and combined, about 3 minutes.

2. Add the strawberry mash, including any accumulated liquid. Beat until combined, 1 to 2 minutes.

3. Add the sugar and beat for another 2 minutes. Taste and adjust the sugar as desired.

4. Scrape the butter into an airtight container and refrigerate until needed. The butter keeps fresh in the refrigerator for about 1 week.

# Sour Cream–Strawberry Waffles

**MAKES ABOUT TEN 3½- BY 4-INCH WAFFLES**

- 3  eggs
- ¾  cup whole milk
- ½  cup (1 stick) butter, melted
- ¾  cup sour cream
- 1  teaspoon vanilla extract
- 1½  cups all-purpose flour
- 2  teaspoons baking powder
- ½  teaspoon baking soda
- ½  teaspoon salt
- 2  cups fresh strawberries, hulled and diced
-  Strawberry Syrup (see below)

*Whether a weekend staple or a breakfast-for-dinner surprise, these waffles are light, fluffy, and crisp. Extra waffles freeze well when tightly wrapped; to serve, reheat in a toaster.*

1. Separate the eggs into two large bowls. Beat the egg whites with an electric hand mixer until stiff, about 3 minutes.

2. Whisk the egg yolks until smooth. Whisk in the milk, butter, sour cream, and vanilla.

3. Whisk together the flour, baking powder, baking soda, and salt in a medium bowl until thoroughly combined, at least 30 seconds. Add to the egg yolk mixture and beat until incorporated. Fold the egg whites into the batter. Scatter 1½ cups of the strawberries over the batter and fold in lightly.

4. Prepare a waffle iron according to the manufacturer's directions and cook the waffles until browned and lightly crispy. Top with the remaining ½ cup fresh strawberries and serve with strawberry syrup.

# Strawberry Syrup

**MAKES 1 CUP**

- 1  pound fresh strawberries, hulled and sliced
- ½  cup water
- ½  cup sugar
- ⅓  cup light corn syrup
- 2  tablespoons lemon juice
-  Pinch of salt

*Drizzle this syrup over pancakes or waffles, pour it over sliced pound cake, or stir it into club soda for a cool drink.*

1. Bring the strawberries, water, sugar, corn syrup, lemon juice, and salt to a boil over high heat in a medium saucepan. Cook for 10 minutes, stirring occasionally. Reduce the heat if necessary to prevent the syrup from boiling over. Remove from the heat when the syrup thickens.

2. Place a metal sieve over a bowl. Strain the strawberry mixture through the sieve, pressing on the solids with the back of a spoon to release all the liquid. Discard the solids or save them for another use. Cool the syrup, then store in the refrigerator for up to 1 week.

# Strawberry Bread with Pecans

**MAKES ONE 9- BY 5-INCH LOAF**

2½ cups all-purpose flour

¾ cups sugar

1 tablespoon baking powder

½ teaspoon salt

⅓ cup butter, cut into ½-inch cubes

¾ cup chopped pecans or other chopped nuts

2 eggs

1 cup milk

1 teaspoon vanilla extract

2 cups fresh strawberries, hulled and diced

*Reminiscent of banana bread, this strawberry bread is moist, dense, and superb with a cup of tea. Substitute any nut you have available.*

1. Preheat the oven to 350°F (180°C). Spray or grease and flour a 9- by 5-inch loaf pan.

2. Whisk together the flour, sugar, baking powder, and salt in a large bowl until thoroughly combined, at least 30 seconds. Scatter the butter cubes over the flour mixture and rub the butter into the flour using your fingers, or cut the butter into the flour with a pastry blender, two knives, or two forks, until the mixture becomes fine crumbs. Toss ½ cup of the nuts into the flour mixture. Make a well in the center of the flour.

3. Whisk the eggs lightly in a medium bowl, and whisk in the milk and vanilla. Add the egg mixture to the well in the flour mixture and stir gently but thoroughly, scraping the bottom of the bowl, until the mixture is just combined. Avoid overmixing. Gently fold the strawberries into the batter.

4. Scoop the batter into the prepared pan and top with the remaining ¼ cup nuts. Bake the bread for about 1 hour 10 minutes, until a toothpick inserted into the center comes out clean (avoiding a strawberry).

5. Let the bread cool in the pan for 10 minutes. Run a knife around the inside edges of the pan to loosen the bread and turn it out onto a wire rack. Slice and serve warm. Refrigerate any leftovers and reheat in a microwave, or toast and slather with butter.

# Small-Batch Refrigerator Strawberry Jam

MAKES ABOUT 1½ CUPS

2 pounds fresh strawberries, hulled and roughly chopped

1 cup sugar

2 tablespoons lemon juice

*Bright summer berries are a gift from nature made into a jam for morning toast, swirled into meringues, or used atop ice cream. Prepared without the fuss of traditional canning, this jam should be stored in the refrigerator and enjoyed within 3 or 4 weeks.*

1. Stir the strawberries, sugar, and lemon juice in a medium saucepan over medium heat. Cook until the berries are bubbling and have begun to soften, 5 to 8 minutes, then reduce the heat to low.

2. Continue cooking until the berries are soft and a spoon leaves a line of separation in the jam when scraping the bottom of the pan, 20 to 25 minutes.

3. Cool and store in clean glass jars or freezer-safe containers.

# Strawberry-Lemon Jam

**MAKES 5 HALF-PINT JARS**

2 pounds hulled fresh strawberries (weigh after hulling)

3 tablespoons low- or no-sugar pectin (like Sure-Jell)

2–2½ cups sugar

1 teaspoon butter

Zest and juice of 3 lemons

*This recipe belongs to my jam-making mentor, Brenda Hill, the Passionate Preserver. She's taught me everything I know about canning. Making jam from scratch is daunting the first time, but the reward is so great that I'm sure you'll make this jam more than once. Homemade jam on a cold winter morning brightens up anyone's day. Do taste a strawberry before beginning. If it's on the sweet side, use 2 cups sugar. If not, use 2½ cups sugar.*

1. To prepare the jars, cover a kitchen counter with a large clean towel. Place a rack in the bottom of a large deep pot with a lid. Add the empty half-pint canning jars without the lids and rings and fill the pot with water, covering the jars by 2 inches. Bring the water to a simmer. Leave the jars simmering until needed, adding additional water as necessary to keep the volume 2 inches higher than the jars. Wash the canning rings and new lids in hot, soapy water and let dry on the towel. Dip a widemouthed funnel into the simmering water and transfer to the towel.

2. While the jars are simmering, place a layer of strawberries in a 2-quart saucepan. Mash the strawberries using a potato masher or other implement. Repeat with more layers until all the berries are mashed. Stir in the pectin, and bring the mixture to a boil over medium-high heat. Add the sugar and stir well until the sugar dissolves. Stir in the butter and lemon zest and juice. Bring to a steady boil (this can take 3 to 5 minutes) and boil hard for 1 minute, stirring constantly and scraping the bottom of the pot. Remove the pot from the heat.

3. Using canning tongs, transfer the jars to the towel. Place a widemouthed funnel in the first jar and carefully ladle hot jam into the jar, leaving ¼-inch headspace. Repeat with the remaining jars. Fold a paper towel and, holding it with standard tongs, dip part of it in the boiling water. Use it to wipe the jar rims free of any drips.

4. Top the jars with lids and rings, tightening the rings with just fingertip strength.

**5.** Return the filled jars to the pot of simmering water, making sure the water covers the jars by 2 inches, and increase the heat to high. When the water is boiling, cover the pot and boil the filled jars for 10 minutes. Remove the pot from the heat, uncover, and let sit for 5 minutes before using canning tongs to transfer the jars to the towel.

**6.** Allow the jars to sit undisturbed for 12 to 24 hours. Remove the rings, check the seals (the lids should be indented, with no leaks, and should not lift off the rim easily), then replace and tighten the rings. Any jars without a tight seal on the lid aren't safe for long-term storage, but they are delightful if refrigerated and consumed in less than 1 month.

# Gluten-Free Strawberry Doughnuts
## *with Strawberry Glaze*

**MAKES 6 DOUGHNUTS**

## Doughnuts

- ¾ cup gluten-free all-purpose flour
- ¼ cup granulated sugar
- ½ teaspoon gluten-free baking powder
- ¼ teaspoon baking soda
- ¼ teaspoon ground cinnamon
- ¼ teaspoon salt
- 1 egg
- ½ cup plain Greek yogurt
- 2 tablespoons milk
- 2 tablespoon canola or other neutral oil
- 6–7 medium fresh strawberries, hulled and diced

## Glaze

- 1 cup confectioners' sugar, sifted
- 2 tablespoons light corn syrup
- 6–7 medium fresh strawberries, hulled, diced, and mashed

*Enjoy fresh, hot doughnuts straight from your own oven. Who could ask for more? Use a commercial one-to-one gluten-free all-purpose flour. You can also use regular all-purpose flour if you don't prefer gluten-free doughnuts. You will need a doughnut pan for this recipe.*

**MAKE THE DOUGHNUTS**

1. Preheat the oven to 350°F (180°C). Spray or grease and flour a six-portion doughnut pan.

2. Whisk the flour, granulated sugar, baking powder, baking soda, cinnamon, and salt together in a large bowl until thoroughly combined, at least 30 seconds.

3. Whisk together the egg, yogurt, milk, and oil in a small bowl. Stir the egg mixture into the flour mixture until just combined. Gently fold in the strawberries.

4. Transfer the mixture to a piping bag or a plastic bag and snip off an end of the bag. Pipe the batter into the prepared doughnut pan molds.

5. Bake the doughnuts for 22 to 25 minutes, until golden brown and a toothpick inserted in the center comes out clean (avoiding a strawberry). Let the pan cool for 5 minutes. Using a small offset spatula if necessary, gingerly transfer the doughnuts to a wire rack to cool.

**MAKE THE GLAZE**

6. While the doughnuts are cooling, stir together the confectioners' sugar, corn syrup, and mashed strawberries in a small bowl until thoroughly combined. Dip one side of each cooled doughnut into the glaze and return to the rack. Dip a second time, if desired. Serve immediately.

# Challah French Toast
## *with Strawberry Syrup*

**MAKES ABOUT 8 SLICES**

8  eggs

4  teaspoons ground cinnamon

1  teaspoon ground allspice

½  teaspoon ground nutmeg

3  tablespoons firmly packed light or dark brown sugar

½  cup whole milk

1  tablespoon vanilla extract

4  tablespoons butter, for cooking

8  slices thick-cut challah bread or French bread

   Confectioners' sugar, for serving

1½  cups fresh strawberries, hulled and sliced

   Strawberry Syrup (page 13), for serving

*This recipe is a family favorite that recalls great memories of our family vacations at the beach with Uncle Rob (my brother-in-law), who would prepare this decadent version. Challah is a braided egg bread well suited to this dish, but sourdough or French bread is a good substitute, if need be.*

1. Preheat the oven to 200°F (95°C). Line a baking sheet with parchment paper.

2. Whisk together the eggs, cinnamon, allspice, nutmeg, and brown sugar in a large wide bowl until the spices are well incorporated. Stir in the milk and vanilla.

3. Heat a large skillet over medium-low heat. Add 1 tablespoon of the butter. Dip two bread slices in the egg batter until completely coated. Add to hot pan and cook until crisp and brown, 3 to 4 minutes. Turn and cook on the second side, 3 to 4 minutes longer. As the slices are cooked, move them to the prepared baking sheet and keep warm in the oven. Repeat with the remaining butter and bread slices.

4. Sprinkle the slices with confectioners' sugar, top with strawberry slices, and drizzle with strawberry syrup. Serve warm.

# Green Strawberry Smoothie Bowl

**MAKES 2 SMOOTHIE BOWLS**

1½ cups frozen strawberries

1 cup baby spinach leaves, loosely packed

¾ cup almond milk

½–¾ cup plain Greek yogurt

1 tablespoon ginger juice

1 tablespoon ground turmeric

½ cup sliced strawberries

½ cup fresh blueberries

1 kiwifruit, peeled and sliced

2 tablespoons mixed chopped nuts

*My daughter, Rachel, is the smoothie queen, and she developed this nutrition-packed breakfast garnished with fruit and nuts. What a great way to start the day!*

1. Combine the frozen strawberries, spinach, almond milk, yogurt, ginger juice, and turmeric in a blender. Whirl for 1 minute, then stop to scrape down the sides of the blender. Continue processing the ingredients until smooth. Divide between two small bowls.

2. Garnish with the sliced strawberries, blueberries, kiwi, and nuts.

# Strawberry Gazpacho

**MAKES 4 SERVINGS**

- 1 cup chopped fresh tomatoes
- 1 cup diced fresh strawberries
- 1 medium cucumber, seeded and roughly chopped
- 1 medium red bell pepper, seeded and roughly chopped
- 1 cup tomato juice
- 1 tablespoon balsamic vinegar
- Salt and freshly ground black pepper
- 1 cup croutons (optional)

*Here's a bowl of thirst-quenching summer flavors. Ripe tomatoes and ripe strawberries are a savory-sweet combination perfect in this modern rendition of the Spanish classic. This recipe doubles easily.*

1. Reserve a small amount of the tomatoes, strawberries, cucumber, and bell pepper for garnish. Place the remaining amounts in a food processor fitted with a metal blade. Add the tomato juice and vinegar, and pulse to combine. Pour the purée into a pitcher or batter bowl with a spout and refrigerate for 2 hours.

2. Before serving, season with salt and black pepper to taste. Pour the gazpacho into individual bowls. Top each serving with the reserved chopped vegetables and strawberries. Garnish with croutons, if desired.

# Hamburger Sliders
### *with Goat Cheese, Strawberries, and Bacon*

**MAKES 6 MINI SLIDERS**

- 6 slider buns
- Butter
- 1 pound ground beef
- ½ teaspoon salt
- ¼ teaspoon freshly ground black pepper
- 1 tablespoon extra-virgin olive oil
- 3 ounces goat cheese
- 2 strips crispy cooked bacon, diced
- 6 medium fresh strawberries, hulled and sliced

*Whether served for lunch, dinner, or a snack, these little burgers are colorful flavor bombs. Alternative cheeses such as blue cheese, sliced cheddar or American, or crumbled feta are all tasty substitutes.*

1. Preheat the oven broiler. Open the slider buns and place them on a baking sheet. Butter the cut sides of the buns. Broil until toasted, about 1 minute, and set aside.

2. Season the ground beef with the salt and pepper in a medium bowl. Combine well and form into six small bun-sized patties.

3. Heat a skillet over medium heat. When hot, drizzle with the oil. Sear the patties for 3 minutes on the first side, turn, and continue to cook until you reach the desired doneness.

4. Spread the goat cheese evenly on the bottom buns. Add the patties and top each with the bacon and strawberries. Cover with the top buns and serve warm.

# Old-Fashioned Strawberry Milkshakes

**MAKES 2 MILKSHAKES**

- 2 cups (1 pint) Rich Strawberry Ice Cream (page 48)
- 6–8 whole strawberries, frozen
- ½–¾ cup milk
- Fresh strawberries, for garnish

*Vanilla and chocolate shakes are always desirable, but a milkshake made with fresh strawberry ice cream is an ethereal pleasure. If using fresh strawberries, hull and freeze for 30 minutes.*

Place the ice cream and frozen strawberries in a blender. Add ½ cup of the milk. Blend just until the strawberries are roughly chopped and the ice cream is smooth. Add additional milk to achieve the desired consistency, if needed. Pour into two glasses, garnish with fresh strawberries, and serve with straws.

# Strawberry Shrub

MAKES 12–14 DRINKS

- 4 cups fresh strawberries, hulled and roughly chopped, plus more for garnish
- 2 cups cider vinegar
- 2 cups sugar
- Ice cubes or crushed ice, for serving
- Cold water or sparkling water, for serving

*The English colonists brought shrubs into the repertoire of American cooks. Developed primarily as a way to preserve fruit before spoiling, this vinegar-based fruit syrup makes a thirst-quenching beverage. Infusing the vinegar with the strawberries for 3 days ensures a full-flavored shrub.*

1. Place the hulled strawberries in a large nonmetallic bowl or container. Add the vinegar, cover tightly, and refrigerate for at least 3 days.

2. Place a sieve over a medium saucepan. Pour the vinegar-marinated strawberries into the sieve, pressing the berries with the back of a spoon to release all the juice. Discard the solids.

3. Add the sugar to the juice and place the saucepan over high heat. Bring to a boil and cook for 3 minutes, stirring occasionally. Remove from the heat and let cool. Pour the sweetened strawberry liquid into a container and chill.

4. To make each drink, add ¼ cup of the strawberry shrub concentrate to a medium glass filled with ice and add 1 cup cold water or sparkling water. Garnish with berries, if desired.

# Strawberry Lemon-Limeade

4 cups fresh strawberries, hulled and halved

½ cup freshly squeezed lemon juice

½ cup freshly squeezed lime juice

4 cups sugar

Ice cubes or crushed ice, for serving

Whole fresh strawberries and sliced lemons and limes, for garnish

*This easy concentrate is smart to have on hand to mix up a cool, refreshing beverage anytime. Use one part concentrate to three parts water.*

1. Combine the halved strawberries, lemon juice, lime juice, and sugar in a medium saucepan over high heat. Bring to a boil and cook until the sugar is dissolved, about 5 minutes, stirring frequently.

2. Place a metal sieve over a bowl. Strain the strawberry mixture through the sieve, pressing on the solids with the back of a spoon to release all the juice. Discard the solids. Transfer the strained concentrate to a jar or container and refrigerate until chilled, about 2 hours.

3. When ready to serve, mix one part concentrate with three parts water. Serve over ice, garnished with strawberries and lemon and lime slices.

# Pork Chops
## *with Strawberry-Balsamic Sauce*

MAKES 4 PORK CHOPS

## Pork Chops

- 4 boneless or bone-in pork chops
- Salt and freshly ground black pepper
- 1 tablespoon extra-virgin olive oil

## Sauce

- 3 cups fresh strawberries, hulled and roughly chopped
- ⅓ cup balsamic vinegar
- 1 tablespoon firmly packed light or dark brown sugar
- Freshly ground black pepper

*Pork chops are ideal for a weeknight supper, and this savory-sweet strawberry sauce turns a plain-Jane chop into the belle of the ball.*

### COOK THE PORK

1. Season the pork chops on both sides with salt and pepper. Heat a large skillet over medium-high heat. Drizzle with the oil. Cook the chops for 3 minutes on the first side, turn, and continue cooking until the second side is browned and the pork is cooked to an internal temperature of at least 145°F (63°C) on an instant-read thermometer, 3 to 4 minutes longer. Transfer the chops to a platter to keep warm.

### MAKE THE SAUCE

2. Return the skillet to the heat and add the strawberries, vinegar, and sugar. Cook, stirring frequently, until the strawberries begin to give off liquid. Taste and season well with pepper. When the mixture has thickened, pour the sauce over the chops and serve warm.

# Strawberry, Burrata, and Arugula Salad

## *with Strawberry-Balsamic Dressing*

**MAKES 4 SERVINGS**

## Salad

- 4 ounces arugula leaves
- 4 ounces burrata
- 1½ cups fresh strawberries, hulled and sliced

## Dressing

- ½ cup fresh strawberries, hulled and halved
- 2 tablespoons balsamic vinegar
- 1 tablespoon honey
- ⅓ cup extra-virgin olive oil
- ½ teaspoon salt
- ¼ teaspoon freshly ground black pepper

*Peppery arugula loves the sweetness of strawberries. Burrata is an Italian cow's-milk cheese with an outside of mozzarella and a creamy center that oozes dairy goodness when cut. Substitute feta or goat cheese as desired.*

**MAKE THE SALAD**

1. Divide the arugula equally among four plates. Top each with one-quarter of the burrata and the strawberries, in that order.

**MAKE THE DRESSING**

2. Place the strawberries, vinegar, honey, oil, salt, and pepper in a blender or food processor and blend until smooth. Drizzle on top of the salads before serving. Store the remaining dressing in a glass jar. Shake well before using.

# Sautéed Chicken Breasts
## *with Strawberry-Onion Jam*

**MAKES 4 SERVING**

### Jam

- 1 tablespoon extra-virgin olive oil
- 2 medium onions, sliced
- ¼ cup balsamic vinegar
- 1 cup chopped fresh strawberries
- 1 cup water
- 1–2 tablespoons firmly packed brown sugar

  Salt and freshly ground black pepper

### Chicken

- 4 boneless, skinless chicken breasts

  Salt and freshly ground black pepper

- 1 tablespoon extra-virgin olive oil

*Strawberry-Onion Jam is a versatile, savory jam that is excellent served over chicken breasts, but it can also be used as a sandwich spread or stirred into soft cheese and served atop crostini as an appetizer. If the chicken breasts are more than a half-inch thick, pound to flatten to an even thickness between pieces of plastic wrap for more even cooking.*

**MAKE THE JAM**

**1.** Heat a large skillet over medium heat. Add the oil and onions, and cook for 2 minutes. Reduce the heat to low and cook the onions until wilted and starting to turn brown, about 20 minutes, stirring occasionally.

**2.** Stir in the vinegar, strawberries, and water. Increase the heat to medium and cook until the strawberries have softened, about 5 minutes. Add the brown sugar, salt, and pepper to taste. Cook until the sugar is dissolved, 1 to 2 minutes. Transfer to a bowl and cover to keep warm.

**COOK THE CHICKEN**

**3.** Wipe out the skillet and increase the heat to medium-high. Season the chicken on both sides with salt and pepper. Pour the oil into the skillet and, when hot, add the chicken breasts and cook for 5 to 7 minutes. Turn the breasts and cook on the second side until browned and cooked through, 5 to 7 minutes longer. The chicken is fully cooked when the thickest part of the breast reaches 165°F (74°C) on an instant-read thermometer.

**4.** Transfer the chicken to a plate and slice. Coat with the jam and serve warm.

# Fish Tacos
## *with Strawberry Salsa*

MAKES 4 TACOS

## Salsa

- 1 pound fresh strawberries, hulled and diced
- ½ medium red onion, finely chopped
- ½ small jalapeño, seeded and minced
- ½ cup cilantro leaves, chopped
- Juice of 2 limes
- Salt

## Avocado Cream

- 2 ripe avocados
- ½ cup sour cream
- Juice of 1 lime
- Salt

## Tacos

- ½ teaspoon ground cumin
- ¼ teaspoon salt
- Pinch of ground chipotle pepper
- 1 pound white fish fillets such as tilapia, grouper, or haddock
- 2 teaspoons extra-virgin olive oil
- 4 flour tortillas
- 2 cups thinly sliced cabbage
- Lime wedges, for serving (optional)

*Switch up taco night with these lively, bright fish tacos drizzled with creamy avocado sauce and topped with fruity salsa.*

### MAKE THE STRAWBERRY SALSA

1. Toss the strawberries, onion, jalapeño, cilantro, and lime juice together in a small bowl and salt to taste. Chill until needed, but not more than 24 hours in advance.

### MAKE THE AVOCADO CREAM

2. Mash the avocados in a small bowl. Stir in the sour cream, lime juice, and salt to taste. Adjust the seasoning, if desired. Chill until needed.

### COMPLETE THE TACOS

3. Stir together the cumin, salt, and chipotle pepper in a small bowl. Season the fish on both sides with the mixture.

4. Heat a skillet over medium heat. When hot, add the oil and fish fillets. Cook the fish on the first side for about 3 minutes, then flip to the second side and cook until the fish is fully cooked through and no longer translucent in the center, 3 to 5 minutes longer, depending on the thickness of the fish. Transfer the fish to a platter.

5. Wipe out the skillet and return it to the heat. When hot, place the tortillas one at a time into the skillet to heat through, then transfer each one to a plate.

6. Assemble the tacos by filling each tortilla with one-quarter of the fish, then topping it with some of the cabbage, salsa, and avocado cream. Serve with lime wedges, if desired.

# Smoked Strawberry Smash

MAKES 1 COCKTAIL

4 fresh strawberries, hulled and halved

3–4 fresh basil leaves, plus more for garnish

3 tablespoons freshly squeezed lime juice

¾ ounce ginger syrup

½ ounce Strawberry Syrup (page 13)

2 ounces mezcal

½ ounce Cointreau

Ice cubes or crushed ice, for serving

*Mezcal, a distilled Mexican liquor, gets its smoky flavor from the roasted hearts of agave plants. It transfers its earthy flavor into this robust beverage. My son, Norman, fancies himself an amateur cocktail maven, and he developed this recipe on a recent trip home to visit. I'm the lucky taste tester.*

Muddle the strawberries, basil, lime juice, and ginger and strawberry syrups in the bottom of a cocktail shaker. Add the mezcal and Cointreau, fill with ice, and shake briefly to combine and chill the ingredients. Pour the liquid and ice into a snifter or collins glass. Garnish with basil leaves, if desired.

# Strawberry Margarita

MAKES 1 COCKTAIL

2 ounces high-quality rum

1 ounce freshly squeezed lime juice

¾ ounce Strawberry Syrup (page 13)

Ice cubes or crushed ice, for serving

Fresh strawberries, for garnish

*The better the rum, the tastier this margarita will be. Sweet and tangy with lime, it's an alcoholic beverage that has earned its place on beach-shack menus and in summer kitchens.*

Combine the rum, lime juice, and strawberry syrup in a cocktail shaker. Fill the shaker with ice and shake briefly to combine and cool the ingredients. Strain into a coupe or other stemmed glass. Garnish with strawberries.

# Skillet Strawberry Cobbler

**MAKES 6 SERVINGS**

- ⅓ cup unsalted butter
- 1 cup self-rising flour
- ½ cup granulated or firmly packed light brown sugar
- 1 cup whole milk
- 4 cups fresh or frozen strawberries, thawed if frozen, hulled and halved

*My go-to dessert when having people over for dinner is this easy cobbler chock-full of strawberry goodness. Assemble the cobbler just before sitting down to dinner, and when dinner is over, the cobbler is ready. Your guests will be impressed! Using brown sugar will result in a darker cobbler.*

1. Preheat the oven to 375°F (190°C). Place the butter in a 10-inch cast-iron skillet and set the skillet in the oven so the butter melts.

2. Whisk the flour and sugar together in a small bowl until thoroughly combined, at least 30 seconds. Whisk in the milk. Remove the hot skillet from the oven and pour the batter onto the hot butter. Sprinkle the strawberries over the top of the batter.

3. Bake the cobbler for 40 to 50 minutes, until the batter has risen around the fruit, the top is light brown, the edges are darker brown, and a toothpick inserted in the center comes out clean (avoiding a strawberry). Serve warm. The cobbler can be made ahead, refrigerated, and reheated before serving.

# Oatmeal-Crumble Strawberry Crisp

**MAKES ABOUT 9 SERVINGS**

- ¾ cup granulated sugar
- 3 tablespoons cornstarch
- 2 pounds fresh strawberries, hulled and quartered
- 1 cup all-purpose flour
- ½ cup old-fashioned rolled oats
- ½ cup firmly packed light brown sugar
- ½ teaspoon ground cinnamon
- ¼ teaspoon salt
- ½ cup (1 stick) butter, melted

  Ice cream, for serving (optional)

*Fruit crisps are a little crunchy on top and gooey-gooey underneath. A warm crisp begs to be served with ice cream. Leftovers qualify for breakfast. Hey, I don't make the rules.*

1. Preheat the oven to 350°F (180°C). Spray a 9-inch square baking pan with cooking spray.

2. Whisk together ¼ cup of the granulated sugar and the cornstarch in a medium bowl. Add the strawberries and toss to coat. Set aside.

3. Whisk together the flour, oats, brown sugar, cinnamon, salt, and the remaining ½ cup granulated sugar in a medium bowl. Drizzle with the butter and stir to combine.

4. Pour the strawberry mixture into the prepared baking pan. Top with the oatmeal mixture, covering the fruit evenly. Bake for about 35 minutes, until the topping is golden brown and the berries are bubbling up. Transfer to a wire rack to cool slightly before serving with ice cream, if desired.

# Rich Strawberry Ice Cream

**MAKES ABOUT 6 CUPS**

- 5 egg yolks
- 1 cup sugar
- 2 cups heavy whipping cream
- 1 cup milk
- 2 tablespoons vanilla extract
- Pinch of salt
- ½ cup Strawberry Jam (page 16 or 18)

*This classic vanilla custard–based ice cream is thick and rich, an excellent base for the ribbon of strawberry jam. For a lighter base, omit the egg yolks and skip the heating.*

**1.** Whisk the egg yolks and sugar together in a small heavy saucepan. Whisk in the cream and milk. Heat over medium heat, stirring every 30 seconds or so, until the temperature of the mixture reads 170°F (77°C) on an instant-read thermometer. Remove from the heat, stir in the vanilla and salt, and pour through a strainer into a container. Refrigerate the custard at least 6 hours, preferably overnight.

**2.** Pour the chilled custard into a prepared ice cream churn and process according to the manufacturer's directions. The ice cream will be soft. Transfer the ice cream to a shallow freezer-safe container. Spread the top with the strawberry jam and run a spatula through the jam into the ice cream to form the ripples. Freeze for at least 6 hours before serving.

# Candied Ginger Shortcake Biscuits
## *with Roasted Strawberries and Cream*

**MAKES SIX 2½-INCH BISCUITS**

## Roasted Strawberries

- 2 pints fresh strawberries, hulled
- 1 teaspoon balsamic vinegar
- 2 tablespoons firmly packed light or dark brown sugar
- Pinch of fine sea salt (optional)

## Biscuits

- 2 cups self-rising flour, plus more for shaping
- 3 tablespoons firmly packed light or dark brown sugar
- ¼ cup diced candied ginger
- 1¼ cups heavy whipping cream, plus 1 tablespoon for brushing
- Decorating sugar or other large-grain sugar

## Whipped Cream

- ½ cup granulated sugar
- Pinch of salt
- 1½ cups heavy whipping cream
- 2 teaspoons vanilla extract

*Although it's yet to be entered in any contests, this summertime classic modernized with candied ginger would surely be a blue-ribbon winner. Warm spicy notes from the ginger, cooled by the sweet brown sugar, make for a special shortcake surprise.*

### ROAST THE STRAWBERRIES

1. Preheat the oven to 375°F (190°C). Line a rimmed baking sheet or sided baking pan with parchment paper.

2. Toss the strawberries and vinegar together in a medium bowl. Sprinkle with the brown sugar and sea salt (if using), and toss lightly.

3. Distribute the strawberries evenly in a single layer in the prepared pan. Roast for 30 minutes. Transfer the strawberries and the juice to a small bowl or container. Use warm, or refrigerate and use within 3 days.

### MAKE THE BISCUITS

4. Set an oven rack to the top position and preheat the oven to 450°F (230°C). Line a baking sheet with parchment paper.

5. Whisk the flour and brown sugar together in a large bowl until thoroughly combined, at least 30 seconds. Toss the ginger into the flour mixture. Pour 1 cup of the cream into the flour and stir with a silicone spatula to quickly pull the flour into the cream. Mix just until the dry ingredients are moistened and the sticky dough begins to pull away from the sides of the bowl. Add a bit of the remaining ¼ cup cream if necessary to incorporate the remaining flour into a shaggy, wettish dough. If the dough is too wet, use more flour when shaping.

**6.** Lightly sprinkle a clean work surface with flour. Turn the dough out onto the floured surface and sprinkle the top of the dough lightly with flour. With floured hands, knead the dough two or three times until it just begins to come together. Fold the dough in half and pat it into a ½-inch-thick rectangle about 5 inches wide and 7½ inches long. Repeat the folding and patting three times, using a little additional flour only if needed, checking to toss flour underneath the dough if necessary to prevent sticking. Brush off any visible flour from the top of the final 5- by 7½-inch rectangle. Using a bench scraper or sharp knife, cut out six 2½-inch square shortcakes.

**7.** Move the shortcakes to the prepared baking sheet, placing them about 2 inches apart. Brush with the 1 tablespoon of cream and sprinkle with decorating sugar. Bake for 6 minutes on the top rack of the oven, then rotate the pan so that the front of the pan is now turned to the back. Bake for 6 to 8 minutes longer, until light golden brown. Transfer to a wire rack to cool.

### PREPARE THE WHIPPED CREAM

**8.** Stir together the granulated sugar and salt in a large deep bowl. Add the cream and vanilla, and beat with an electric hand mixer until the cream has thickened and holds a firm peak, about 3 minutes. The cream may be made up to 8 hours ahead and stored in the refrigerator.

### ASSEMBLE THE SHORTCAKES

**9.** Split the shortcakes open and pile roasted strawberries on the bottom half. Add a small dollop of whipped cream, cover with the top of the shortcakes, and top with another dollop of whipped cream. Extra shortcakes freeze well, wrapped tightly, for up to 2 months.

# Diner-Style Fresh Strawberry Pie

**MAKES ONE 9-INCH PIE**

1 refrigerated piecrust

10 cups fresh strawberries, hulled, plus more for garnish

⅔ cup sugar

3 tablespoons cornstarch

2 tablespoons lemon juice

2 cups heavy whipping cream

*It takes a gracious plenty of strawberries to make a diner-style fresh strawberry pie piled high with ripe fruit and topped with whipped cream. Larger berries are particularly desirable in this pie for a lush, ample appearance.*

1. Let the piecrust rest at room temperature for about 15 minutes, or according to package directions. Line a 9-inch pie pan with the crust and finish the edges as desired. Prebake the piecrust according to package directions. Cool until needed.

2. Inspect the strawberries and cut any extra-large berries into halves or quarters. Reserve a few berries for garnish, if desired.

3. Place 2½ cups of the strawberries in a large saucepan. Crush the berries using a potato masher or other implement. Whisk together 2 tablespoons of the sugar and the cornstarch in a small bowl, and add to the strawberries in the pot. Cook over medium heat until the sugar is dissolved and the mixture is thickened, about 10 minutes, stirring well. Remove from the heat and stir in the lemon juice.

4. While the berry mixture is cooling, whip the cream and the remaining sugar in a large deep bowl using an electric hand mixer until stiff peaks form, about 4 minutes.

5. Place the remaining 7½ cups berries in a large bowl and mix in the cooked berries, stirring well to reach all the berries. Pour the berries into the cooled pie shell.

6. Pile the whipped cream over the pie and refrigerate until firm, about 2 hours. When serving, garnish the cut slices with additional fresh berries, if desired.

# Pink Strawberry Pie

*with Lattice Crust*

**MAKES ONE 9-INCH PIE**

## Crust

- ½ cup freeze-dried strawberries
- 1 tablespoon granulated sugar
- 2½ cups all-purpose flour, plus more for rolling
- ½ teaspoon salt
- 1 cup (2 sticks) salted butter, cut into ½-inch cubes
- 8–10 tablespoons ice-cold water
- 1 egg white, lightly beaten
- 1 tablespoon cool water
- 2 tablespoons decorating sugar or other large-grain sugar

## Filling

- ½ cup granulated sugar
- ⅓ cup cornstarch
- ¼ teaspoon salt
- 5–6 cups fresh strawberries, hulled and chopped
- 1 tablespoon lemon juice

*Freeze-dried strawberries add extra flavor to this showstoppingly beautiful pie. This crust comes from a beloved family recipe belonging to cookbook author and my friend Cathy Barrow. It is butter-rich, making it an easy crust for beginners. Refrigerating the dough for 1 hour allows the gluten to relax and makes the dough easier to roll.*

**MAKE THE CRUST**

1. Place the freeze-dried strawberries and granulated sugar in a food processor fitted with a metal blade. Pulse into a fine powder. Add the flour and salt, and pulse 2 or 3 times to mix. Distribute the butter cubes evenly over the flour mixture. Pulse 15 times. Add 4 tablespoons of the cold water. Pulse 10 times. Add 4 more tablespoons of the cold water and pulse 5 times. Grab a pinch of dough and squeeze it together. If it crumbles, add the remaining 2 tablespoons of water to bring the dough together. Turn the dough out onto a floured board. Knead slightly to form a cohesive dough. Divide the dough in half, form into two 5-inch disks, wrap each in plastic wrap, and refrigerate for at least 1 hour.

**MAKE THE FILLING**

2. Whisk the granulated sugar, cornstarch, and salt together in a small bowl. Toss the strawberries with the lemon juice in a large bowl. Sprinkle the strawberries with the cornstarch mixture and toss until the berries are evenly coated.

## ASSEMBLE THE PIE

3. Preheat the oven to 425°F (220°C).

4. Remove the dough from the refrigerator and let rest for 10 minutes. Dust a work surface and rolling pin with flour. Roll out one disk, working from the center out to the edge, then pick up the rolling pin and turn the dough a quarter turn. Repeat, beginning in the center each time and turning the dough after each roll, until the dough is roughly 1 inch larger than what will line a 9-inch pie pan. Move the dough gently to the pan. Fill the crust with the strawberry mixture and refrigerate.

5. Roll out the second disk. Cut the dough into 1- to 1½-inch-wide strips. Remove the pie from the refrigerator and weave the strips to form a lattice on top of the pie, as shown in the photos at right. Seal the edges between the lattice strips and bottom dough with a dab of water, and tuck the long strips under the edge of the dough. Whisk the egg white and cool water together in a small bowl, then brush the lattice with the egg wash. If this process has warmed up the piecrust, move the whole pie to the refrigerator until the dough is firm, about 20 minutes.

6. Transfer the pie to a rimmed baking sheet. Bake for 20 minutes. Reduce the heat to 350°F (180°C) and bake for 30 minutes. If the crust is browning too quickly, cover the edges loosely with aluminum foil. Sprinkle the pie with decorating sugar and bake for 10 minutes longer, or until browned as desired. Let cool completely before cutting.

Step 5a

Step 5b

Step 5c

# Strawberry Heart Hand Pies

**MAKES ABOUT TEN 2½-INCH HAND PIES**

- 1 package (2-count) refrigerated piecrusts
- 2 tablespoons granulated sugar
- 1 tablespoon cornstarch
- ½ cup finely diced fresh strawberries
- All-purpose flour, for dusting the work surface
- 1 egg white, lightly beaten
- 1 tablespoon water
- Decorating sugar or other large-grain sugar

*Show your love with these heart-shaped hand pies as a valentine for any month of the year.*

1. Let the piecrusts rest at room temperature for about 15 minutes, or according to package directions. Line a baking sheet with parchment paper.

2. Whisk together the granulated sugar and cornstarch in a small bowl. Add the strawberries and toss to coat.

3. Lightly flour a work surface. Gently roll out the piecrusts. Using a 2½-inch-long heart-shaped cookie cutter, cut hearts out of both crusts (about 20 hearts total). Move half of the heart crusts to the prepared baking sheet, spacing them 1 to 2 inches apart. Using a small heart-shaped cutter, cut out a center heart from each of the remaining hearts. Discard these little centers or sprinkle with sugar and bake along with the hand pies for a cook's treat.

4. Place 1 rounded teaspoonful of the strawberry mixture in the center of each heart on the baking sheet. Dampen the edges of the hearts with a fingertip dipped in water and top with the remaining hearts that have the cut-outs, pressing the edges to seal. Crimp the edges with a fork.

5. Whisk the egg white and water together in a small bowl. Brush the pies with the egg wash. Sprinkle with decorating sugar and freeze the pies for 10 minutes.

6. Meanwhile, preheat the oven to 400°F (200°C).

7. Bake the pies for about 20 minutes, until lightly browned. Cool for 10 minutes. Serve warm or at room temperature. Store in an airtight container for up to 2 days.

# Shortbread Tart
## *with Strawberries and Pastry Cream*

**MAKES ONE 9- OR 10-INCH TART**

### Pastry Cream

- ½ cup sugar
- ¼ cup cornstarch
- Pinch of salt
- 4 egg yolks
- 2 cups whole milk
- 1 teaspoon vanilla extract

### Shortbread

- 1¼ cups all-purpose flour
- ⅓ cup sugar
- ¼ teaspoon salt
- 10 tablespoons unsalted butter, at room temperature
- 1 teaspoon vanilla extract
- 1–2 teaspoons milk (optional)

### Finish

- ⅓ cup red currant jelly or other clear jelly
- 1 quart fresh strawberries, hulled and sliced

*Pastry cream is a rich custard that makes a luxurious filling for this sweet shortbread-crusted tart. The glistening glaze makes the strawberries sparkle.*

**MAKE THE PASTRY CREAM**

1. Whisk together the sugar, cornstarch, and salt in a large saucepan. Whisk in the egg yolks until smooth. Stir in ½ cup of the milk and whisk until smooth. Stir in the remaining 1½ cups milk. Heat the saucepan over medium heat, stirring constantly and scraping the bottom and sides of the pan with a silicone spatula, until the mixture thickens, about 5 minutes. Remove from the heat and stir in the vanilla. Cover the surface of the custard with a sheet of plastic wrap, let cool to room temperature, and refrigerate for 4 hours.

**MAKE THE SHORTBREAD**

2. While the pastry cream is chilling, whisk together the flour, sugar, and salt in a large deep bowl. Add the butter and vanilla, and beat with an electric hand mixer until the mixture comes together as a cohesive dough, 2 to 3 minutes. The dough takes time to come together, so be patient. If it hasn't come together after 3 minutes, add a teaspoon or two of milk until the dough forms a clump. Pat the dough into the bottom of a 9- or 10-inch round tart pan with a removable bottom. Place the pan on a rimmed baking sheet and refrigerate for 1 hour.

3. Preheat the oven to 350°F (180°C).

4. Bake the chilled crust for about 20 minutes, or until golden. Transfer to a wire rack to cool completely. When cool, wrap in plastic wrap until needed.

## FINISH THE TART

**5.** Heat the jelly in a small saucepan over low heat until just melted. Spread the pastry cream over the tart. Top with the sliced strawberries. Brush with the melted jelly. Chill the finished tart for about 1 hour before serving. Refrigerate any leftovers.

# Rustic Strawberry Galette

**MAKES ONE 8- TO 9-INCH GALETTE**

1 refrigerated piecrust

4 cups fresh strawberries, hulled, and halved if large

¼ cup honey, warmed slightly

1 tablespoon cornstarch

1 teaspoon vanilla extract

All-purpose flour, for dusting the work surface

⅓ cup Strawberry Jam (page 16 or 18)

1 egg yolk

1 tablespoon heavy whipping cream

Decorating sugar or other large-grain sugar

*Free-form tarts, also called galettes, are easy, rustic pies that signal a more relaxed, less fussy end to a meal. Premade piecrusts make it easy.*

**1.** Let the piecrust rest at room temperature for about 15 minutes, or according to package directions. Line a baking sheet with parchment paper.

**2.** Toss the strawberries, honey, cornstarch, and vanilla together in a medium bowl.

**3.** Lightly flour a work surface. Roll out the piecrust into a 10-inch round and transfer to the prepared baking sheet. Spread the dough with the jam, leaving a 1-inch border around the edge. Using a slotted spoon, distribute the berry mixture over the jam in an even layer. Discard or reserve any remaining liquid in the bowl (see note). Fold up the crust edges to extend over the berries, pleating every inch or two as needed to keep the shape.

**4.** Whisk the egg yolk and cream together in a small bowl. Brush the dough with the egg mixture and sprinkle with decorating sugar. Move the baking sheet with the galette to the refrigerator and chill for 30 minutes.

**5.** Meanwhile, preheat the oven to 400°F (200°C).

**6.** Bake the chilled galette on the baking sheet for 45 to 50 minutes, or until golden brown. The galette may weep liquid from the strawberries in the crust, which discolors the parchment. It looks messy, but the galette itself is delicious! Cool slightly on a wire rack, then carefully transfer to a platter for serving.

**Note:** The leftover liquid from the berry mixture makes a tasty topping for ice cream. Simply bring it to a boil in a small saucepan and cook until thickened. Cool and refrigerate until needed.

# Stunning Strawberry Summer Birthday Cake

## *with Pink Marshmallow Buttercream*

**MAKES ONE 8-INCH
THREE-LAYER CAKE**

## Cake

2¼ cups granulated sugar

1 cup (2 sticks) unsalted
butter, at room temperature

3 eggs, at room temperature

1 tablespoon vanilla extract

3½ cups all-purpose flour

4½ teaspoons baking powder

1 teaspoon salt

2 cups milk, at room
temperature

1 pint fresh strawberries,
hulled and sliced

## Buttercream

½ cup freeze-dried
strawberries

2⅓ cups confectioners' sugar

2 cups (4 sticks) unsalted
butter, at room temperature

½ teaspoon salt

1 (16-ounce) jar
marshmallow creme

*Pink frosting has long been a birthday cake must for my daughter, Rachel. This traditional vanilla cake is a stunner — grand in height and superlative in taste. Plan ahead to set out the ingredients to bring them to room temperature before beginning.*

**MAKE THE CAKE**

1. Preheat the oven to 350°F (180°C). Spray or grease and flour three 8-inch round cake pans and line with parchment paper. If only two pans are available, bake according to the following directions, reserving the last batch of batter at room temperature, and bake the third layer as soon as a pan is available.

2. Beat the granulated sugar and butter together in a large deep bowl with an electric hand mixer until light and fluffy, 5 to 6 minutes, stopping once to scrape down the sides of the bowl with a spatula.

3. Add the eggs one at a time, beating after each addition until incorporated. Beat in the vanilla.

4. Whisk together the flour, baking powder, and salt in a small bowl until thoroughly combined, at least 30 seconds.

5. Add the flour to the butter mixture in thirds, alternating with half the milk, beating until combined and scraping the bottom of the bowl between each addition.

6. Divide the batter evenly between the three prepared pans. Firmly tap each of the pans on the counter once to release any air bubbles.

**7.** Bake the cakes for 30 to 33 minutes, until puffed up, firm, and light colored and a toothpick inserted in the center comes out clean. If only two pans fit in the oven, leave the third aside and bake after the first two are finished. Transfer the layers to a wire rack, run an offset spatula around the inside edges of the pans, and let cool for 1 hour. Invert the layers onto the rack, remove the parchment, and turn the layers right-side up. The cake layers freeze beautifully, without frosting, if well wrapped.

## MAKE THE BUTTERCREAM

**8.** While the layers are cooling, place the freeze-dried strawberries and confectioners' sugar in a food processor fitted with a metal blade. Pulse into a fine powder. Move to a large deep bowl. Add the butter and salt, and beat with an electric hand mixer until smooth, about 1 minute. Add the marshmallow creme and beat until light and fluffy, about 5 minutes, scraping the bowl with a spatula as needed.

## ASSEMBLE AND FROST THE CAKE

**9.** Trim the layers with a serrated knife to achieve a flat top. Reserve the scraps for a cook's treat!

**10.** Place a single dab of frosting on a cake platter to keep the cake stable. Move the first layer to the platter. Frost the top of the first layer and cover it with some of the sliced strawberries. Add the second layer and repeat. Top with the third layer. Frost the top and sides of the cake, swirling the frosting as desired for a decorative finish.

**11.** The cake is fine at room temperature the day it is made and served. After the first day, move the cake to the refrigerator. The frosting will firm, so it's best to allow slices cut later to come to room temperature for about 1 hour before serving.

# Strawberry Creamsicles

**MAKES 12**

2 cups heavy whipping cream

1 cup sugar

4 cups fresh strawberries, hulled and finely chopped

*Childhood isn't complete without the joy of a creamsicle. Freezer-safe silicone molds are among the numerous choices available that come complete with disposable wooden or reusable sticks. Halve this recipe if your mold is small.*

1. Place an ice-pop mold on a baking sheet. Prepare space for it in the freezer.

2. Whip the cream in a large deep bowl with an electric hand mixer for about 1 minute. Add the sugar and continue whipping until stiff peaks form, 4 to 5 minutes. Fold the strawberries into the whipped cream. Transfer the mixture to a large ziplock plastic bag. Snip a bottom corner of the bag.

3. Insert the snipped corner of the bag down into one of the ice-pop molds. Squeeze the mixture into the bottom of the mold and lift the bag up, still squeezing, to fill the mold. Repeat with the remaining molds. Set in the sticks according to the manufacturer's directions, as some molds come with slatted lids and others do not. Transfer the mold on the baking sheet to the freezer and freeze until solid, usually 4 to 5 hours.

4. To serve, run cold water along the outside of the mold. Lightly squeeze the pops up and out of the molds. Serve immediately.

# Strawberry-Pistachio Bundt Cake
## *with Lemon Glaze*

**MAKES ONE 10- OR 12-INCH BUNDT CAKE**

## Cake

- 3 cups all-purpose flour, plus more for dusting the pan
- 2 cups granulated sugar
- 1 teaspoon lemon zest
- 1 cup (2 sticks) unsalted butter, at room temperature
- 4 eggs, at room temperature
- 2 teaspoons vanilla extract
- 1 teaspoon baking soda
- ½ teaspoon baking powder
- ½ teaspoon salt
- ⅔ cup buttermilk
- 1½ cups fresh strawberries, hulled and sliced
- ¾ cup chopped pistachios

## Glaze

- 1½ cups confectioners' sugar
- ¼ cup freshly squeezed lemon juice

*Fluted tube pans are designed to handle thick, pound-cake-like batters, allowing the cake to cook thoroughly. This dense batter rewards the taste buds with a rich cake studded with nuts and strawberries, finished with a glistening lemony glaze. Coat the inside of the pan diligently to prevent sticking. If a piece of cake does stick, release it with a blunt knife and move it into place. Cover with glaze to hide any imperfections.*

**MAKE THE CAKE**

1. Set an oven rack at the lowest level in the oven. Preheat the oven to 350°F (180°C). Spray or grease the inside of a 10- to 12-cup Bundt pan with oil and dust with flour.

2. Use your fingers to rub together the granulated sugar and lemon zest in a large deep bowl until thoroughly combined. Add the butter and beat with an electric hand mixer until light in color and fluffy, 3 to 4 minutes. Add the eggs one at a time, beating after each addition until incorporated. Beat in the vanilla.

3. Whisk together the flour, baking soda, baking powder, and salt in a small bowl until thoroughly combined, at least 30 seconds.

4. Add the flour mixture to the butter mixture in thirds, alternating with half the buttermilk, beating until combined and scraping the bottom of the bowl between each addition. Gently fold in the strawberries and pistachios.

5. Spread the batter in the prepared pan, and tap the pan on the counter once or twice to remove any air bubbles. Move the pan to a baking sheet and place on the bottom rack in the hot oven.

**6.** Bake for 65 to 70 minutes, or until the cake is golden brown on top, begins to pull away a bit from the sides of the pan, and a toothpick inserted in the center comes out clean (avoiding a strawberry). Let cool on a wire rack for 1 hour. Invert the cake onto the rack to finish cooling. Transfer the cake to a serving platter. Or, to freeze the cake, wrap the unglazed cake well and store in the freezer for up to 3 months, then glaze at serving time.

## MAKE THE GLAZE

**7.** Mix together the confectioners' sugar and lemon juice in a small bowl. If the glaze is too thick, add a little water until you achieve the desired consistency. Drizzle the glaze over the cooled cake.

# Strawberry Cream–Filled Chocolate Roll

## *with Chocolate Ganache*

## Roll

- ½ cup all-purpose flour
- ¼ cup unsweetened cocoa powder
- 1 teaspoon baking powder
- ½ teaspoon salt
- 4 eggs
- ½ cup granulated sugar
- 2 tablespoons butter, melted
- 1 teaspoon vanilla extract

## Strawberry Cream

- ½ cup freeze-dried strawberries
- 1 cup confectioners' sugar
- 1 (8-ounce) package cream cheese
- ½ teaspoon vanilla extract
- ½ teaspoon salt
- 1 cup heavy whipping cream
- ⅓ cup finely chopped fresh strawberries

*Thin chocolate cake spread with strawberry cream and rolled into a spiral log, drizzled with chocolate topping, makes a stunning dessert centerpiece. Hashtag this confection as a #masterpiece.*

**MAKE THE CHOCOLATE ROLL**

1. Preheat the oven to 350°F (180°C). Spray a 10- by 15-inch jelly roll pan with cooking spray and line with parchment paper, extending the paper by at least 1 inch on either end. Spray the paper. Cover a wire rack with a clean kitchen towel and set aside.

2. Whisk together the flour, cocoa powder, baking powder, and salt in a medium bowl until thoroughly combined, at least 30 seconds.

3. Whisk the eggs and granulated sugar together in a large bowl until thick, about 1 minute. Whisk in the butter and vanilla. Fold in the flour mixture until just combined.

4. Spread the batter evenly in the prepared pan. Bake for 10 to 11 minutes, or until the top of the cake springs back. The cake cooks quickly, as it is so thin. Remove the pan from the oven, and invert onto prepared rack.

5. Roll the cake and parchment from short end to short end. Set it seam-side down and let fully cool.

**PREPARE THE STRAWBERRY CREAM**

6. While the cake is cooling, place the freeze-dried strawberries and ¾ cup of the confectioners' sugar in a food processor fitted with a metal blade and pulse into a fine powder. Move to a large deep bowl. Add the cream cheese and beat with an electric hand mixer until smooth. Beat in the vanilla and salt.

**7.** Whip the cream in a second large deep bowl, using an electric hand mixer, for about 1 minute. Add the remaining ¼ cup confectioners' sugar and whip until stiff peaks form, about 3 minutes.

**8.** Fold three-quarters of the whipped cream into the cream cheese mixture, reserving the remaining whipped cream for the topping. Gently fold the chopped strawberries into the cream cheese mixture.

**9.** Carefully unroll the cake. It won't unroll flat, but spread the filling evenly over the surface, leaving a ½-inch border. Carefully reroll the cake, gently peeling away the parchment. Discard the parchment. Secure the roll in plastic wrap and refrigerate at least 1 hour.

**MAKE THE CHOCOLATE GANACHE**

**10.** When ready to serve, combine the cream, corn syrup, and chocolate chips in a small saucepan over medium-low heat and warm until the chocolate is melted and fully incorporated, stirring until it is silky smooth.

**11.** Move the roll, seam-side down, onto a serving platter, discarding the plastic wrap. Trim both ends of the cake with a serrated knife for a professional appearance. Slowly pour the ganache over the cake, allowing it to drip. Top with the remaining whipped cream and garnish with the whole strawberries. Cut into slices for serving. Refrigerate any leftovers.

## Ganache

- ½ cup heavy whipping cream
- 2 tablespoons light corn syrup
- 1 cup semisweet chocolate chips
- 3–4 large whole fresh strawberries, for garnish

# Strawberry-Mint Sorbet

**MAKES ABOUT 6 CUPS**

- 1½ cups water
- 1½ cups sugar
- 20 leaves fresh mint, no stems, plus some small leaves for garnish
- 2½ pounds fresh strawberries, hulled

*Frosty, sweet, and smooth, this scarlet sorbet is an impressive dessert after dinner, or a cooling afternoon treat.*

1. Heat the water and sugar together in a medium saucepan over medium-high heat. Bring to a boil, then reduce to a simmer. Cook for 10 minutes. Remove from the heat.

2. Lightly bruise the mint leaves by rubbing between your fingers or pounding, then add to the syrup. Let cool.

3. When the syrup is cool, remove the mint leaves, then pour the syrup into a blender or a food processor fitted with a metal blade. Add the strawberries and purée. Place a metal sieve over a large bowl and strain the strawberry mixture into the bowl. Place the mixture in the refrigerator and chill for 2 hours, or until thoroughly chilled.

4. Pour the chilled mixture into a prepared ice cream churn and process according to the manufacturer's directions. The sorbet will be soft. Transfer the sorbet to a shallow freezer-safe container. Freeze for at least 6 hours before serving. Garnish with the reserved small mint leaves.

# Chocolate Cupcakes
## *with Strawberry Frosting*

## Cupcakes

- 1 cup all-purpose flour
- ½ cup unsweetened cocoa powder
- 1 teaspoon baking powder
- ½ teaspoon baking soda
- ¼ teaspoon salt
- ½ cup canola or other neutral oil
- 1 cup granulated sugar
- 1 teaspoon vanilla extract
- 2 eggs
- ½ cup buttermilk

## Frosting

- 1½ cups fresh strawberries, hulled and chopped
- 1 cup (2 sticks) unsalted butter, at room temperature
- 4–5 cups confectioners' sugar, plus more for garnish
- 1–2 tablespoons heavy whipping cream
- ½ cup mini chocolate chips, for garnish (optional)

*Chocolate cupcakes make everyone feel like a little kid again, and this recipe yields moist, rich cake with a subtly sweet and delightfully pink frosting sure to please. My student Grace developed this recipe.*

### MAKE THE CUPCAKES

1. Preheat the oven to 350°F (185°C). Line a 12-cup muffin pan with paper cup liners, or spray the pan with cooking spray.

2. Whisk the flour, cocoa powder, baking powder, baking soda, and salt together in a small bowl until thoroughly combined, at least 30 seconds.

3. Beat together the oil, granulated sugar, vanilla, and eggs in a large bowl with an electric hand mixer until combined, about 1 minute.

4. Add the flour mixture to the sugar mixture in thirds, alternating with half the buttermilk, beating until combined and scraping the bottom of the bowl between each addition.

5. Spoon the batter into the prepared muffin pan, filling each cup about two-thirds full. Bake for 15 to 18 minutes, until a toothpick inserted in the center comes out clean.

### MAKE THE FROSTING

6. While the cupcakes are baking, place the strawberries in a food processor fitted with a metal blade and purée. Set a metal sieve over a small saucepan and transfer the purée to the sieve. Using the back of a spoon, press the purée to remove the seeds. Place the saucepan over low heat and bring to a gentle boil, stirring occasionally to prevent burning. Boil until the mixture is thick like jam and reduced to ⅓ to ¼ cup, about 15 minutes. Using a silicone spatula, scrape the purée into a shallow container and refrigerate until completely cooled.

**7.** When the purée is cool, beat the butter in a large deep bowl until fluffy. Beat in 2 cups of the confectioners' sugar. Beat in 3 or 4 tablespoons of the purée. Beat in the remaining 2 to 3 cups confectioners' sugar, about ½ cup at a time, until the desired consistency is reached. Add 1 to 2 tablespoons of the cream as needed to achieve a spreadable consistency.

**8.** Frost the cupcakes using a piping bag and tip, or a knife. Garnish with mini chocolate chips, if desired.

# Strawberry Meringue Stack Cake

**MAKES ONE 8-INCH
THREE-LAYER CAKE**

6  egg whites

1  teaspoon lemon juice

2  tablespoons cornstarch

   Pinch of salt

2  cups sugar

2  cups heavy whipping cream

4  cups fresh strawberries,
   hulled and sliced, plus a
   few whole for garnish

*Presentation is everything for this gorgeous cake. Be
sure to grab a photo before slicing, as it doesn't slice
well, but its taste more than makes up for the lack of a
photogenic serving. Meringue is best made on a dry day.
Humidity inhibits the egg white's ability to dry out, and
it will weep and be sticky.*

**1.** Preheat the oven to 250°F (120°C). Line two baking
sheets with parchment paper. Draw two 8-inch circles
on one sheet and one 8-inch circle on the other. Dab the
parchment with a few drops of oil. Invert the papers onto
the baking sheets, marked sides down.

**2.** Beat the egg whites and lemon juice together in a
large deep bowl with an electric hand mixer until foamy,
about 1 minute. Add the cornstarch and salt. Gradually add
1½ cups of the sugar, 1 tablespoon at a time, beating on
medium-high until stiff peaks form and the egg whites turn
into a glossy meringue, about 4 minutes.

**3.** Using an offset spatula, spread one-third of the
meringue mixture on each of the three circles.

**4.** Bake the meringues for 1 hour, switching the baking
sheets on the oven racks halfway through the baking time.
Turn the oven off and leave the meringues in the oven until
dry, about 2½ hours.

**5.** To assemble the cake, whip the cream in a large deep
bowl with an electric hand mixer, about 1 minute. Add the
remaining ½ cup sugar and continue whipping until stiff
peaks form, 4 to 5 minutes.

**6.** Place a small dollop of whipped cream in the center of a cake stand to help secure the cake. Move one meringue layer to the cake stand. Spread one-third of the whipped cream over the first layer. Top with one-third of the strawberries. Add the second layer and repeat. Add the third layer and repeat, adding the extra whole strawberries to garnish.

**7.** The cake is best served immediately after assembly. It can be chilled up to 2 hours, if needed. The leftovers become soggy but are still tasty if refrigerated and eaten the next day.

# Instant Pot Cheesecake
## *with Chocolate Crust and Strawberry Sauce*

**MAKES ONE 7-INCH CHEESECAKE**

## Sauce

- 2 cups fresh or frozen strawberries (thawed if frozen, saving the juices)
- 1 tablespoon lemon juice
- ⅓ cup sugar
- 1 tablespoon cornstarch
- 1 tablespoon finely ground freeze-dried strawberries (optional)

## Crust

- 2 cups crushed Oreo cookies (about one 10-ounce package; see note)
- 2 tablespoons unsalted butter, melted

**Note:** To crush the cookies, place them in a ziplock plastic bag and seal. Crush with a rolling pin, or your hands, until fine crumbs form.

*Making cheesecake in a 6- or 8-quart Instant Pot pressure cooker alleviates the stress of watching a cheesecake bake in the oven, waiting to see if it cracks. Not only does this method eliminate that tension, it has a sauce that would cover any crack that might form. Oreo cookies are ideal for this crust. Scrape the filling out of at least half the cookies before crushing (Oreo Thins can be used as they are).*

1. Fold a 24-inch-long piece of foil in half lengthwise and in half again lengthwise, to form a foil sling 3 inches wide and about 24 inches long. Place a wire rack or metal trivet on the bottom of the Instant Pot insert.

### MAKE THE SAUCE

2. Combine the fresh or frozen strawberries and lemon juice in a small saucepan over medium heat. Whisk together the sugar and cornstarch in a small bowl, and add to strawberries. Stir in the freeze-dried strawberries, if using. Bring the mixture to a boil, reduce the heat to low, and crush the strawberries with a potato masher or other implement. Simmer until the mixture thickens, about 5 minutes. Let cool.

3. Place the sauce mixture in a blender or a food processor fitted with a metal blade and purée. Place ⅓ cup of the sauce in a shallow bowl and refrigerate. Refrigerate the remaining sauce separately until serving.

### MAKE THE CRUST

4. Place the cookie crumbs in a small bowl, pour in the butter, and combine thoroughly with a fork. Press the crumbs into the bottom of a 7-inch springform pan, completely and evenly covering the bottom. Use the bottom of a glass to smooth the surface. The smoother the edges, the cleaner the appearance of the line between the filling and crust will be in the finished cake. Transfer the pan to the freezer until needed.

## MAKE THE FILLING

**5.** Beat the cream cheese and sour cream together in a large bowl with an electric hand mixer until just combined. Add the eggs one at a time, beating and scraping the bowl after each addition. Stir in the cornstarch, sugar, lemon juice, and vanilla. Fold in the reserved ⅓ cup strawberry sauce, turning it in completely for a pink cheesecake, or folding it in lightly for a pink swirl effect.

## ASSEMBLE THE CAKE

**6.** Remove the crust from the freezer and pour the cheesecake filling into the crust. Smooth the top with an offset spatula, if needed.

**7.** Pour 1 cup water into the Instant Pot insert. Place the springform pan in the center of the foil sling and move the sling and pan into an 8-inch cake pan. (If your Instant Pot is smaller than 8 quarts, wrap the bottom of the springform pan with aluminum foil instead.) Move the cake pan onto the rack inside the insert. Tuck the sling into the sides.

**8.** Seal the top of the pot and cook on high pressure for 25 minutes. Allow for a natural release for 15 minutes, then switch to manual release. Remove the lid carefully to avoid dripping moisture onto the cheesecake. Use the sling to remove the springform pan. Dab the top of the cheesecake lightly with paper towels if necessary to remove any collected moisture. Let the cheesecake cool for 30 minutes at room temperature, then move the cheesecake to the refrigerator for at least 6 hours, but preferably overnight.

**9.** When ready to serve, remove the cheesecake from the refrigerator. Run an offset spatula around the inside edge of the pan. Open the springform pan and transfer the cheesecake to a serving platter. Top the cheesecake with the remaining cooled sauce. Cut and serve.

## Filling

- 2 (8-ounce) packages cream cheese, at room temperature
- ¼ cup sour cream
- 2 eggs, at room temperature
- 1 tablespoon cornstarch
- ½ cup sugar
- 2 teaspoons lemon juice
- 1 teaspoon vanilla extract

# No-Bake Pecan-Crusted Strawberry Cheesecake Bars

## *with Strawberry Sauce*

MAKES SIXTEEN 2-INCH
SQUARES

---

### Crust

1½  cups graham cracker
      crumbs

½  cup finely ground pecans

2  tablespoons sugar

½  cup (1 stick)  butter, melted

### Sauce

2  cups fresh or frozen
    strawberries (thawed if
    frozen, saving the juices)

1  tablespoon lemon juice

⅓  cup sugar

1  tablespoon cornstarch

1  tablespoon finely ground
    freeze-dried strawberries
    (optional)

### Filling

2  (8-ounce) packages
    cream cheese, at room
    temperature

1  cup sugar

1½  cups fresh strawberries,
      hulled and sliced

½  cup heavy whipping cream

1  teaspoon vanilla extract

*Creamy and cool, these sweet cheesecake bites are easy to make and perfect on hot summer days when you don't want to heat the oven. The parchment is essential for keeping the crust intact. Substitute other nuts as desired.*

**MAKE THE CRUST**

1. Line an 8-inch square baking pan with parchment paper, leaving at least a 1-inch overhang on all sides.

2. Whisk together the graham cracker crumbs, pecans, and sugar in a small bowl. Stir in the butter until thoroughly combined. Pat the mixture into the prepared pan and refrigerate for 1 hour.

**PREPARE THE SAUCE**

3. While the crust is cooling, combine the fresh or frozen strawberries and lemon juice in a small saucepan over medium heat. Whisk together the sugar and cornstarch in a small bowl, and add to the strawberries. Stir in the freeze-dried strawberries, if using. Bring the mixture to a boil, reduce the heat to low, and crush the strawberries with a potato masher or other implement. Simmer until the mixture thickens, about 5 minutes. Let cool. Place the sauce mixture in a blender or a food processor fitted with a metal blade and purée. Transfer the sauce to an airtight container and refrigerate until ready to serve.

**MAKE THE FILLING**

4. Beat the cream cheese and sugar together in a large deep bowl using an electric hand mixer until smooth, about 1 minute. Stir in the strawberries.

**5.** Whip the cream and vanilla in a deep bowl until stiff peaks form, 3 to 4 minutes. Fold half of the whipped cream into the cream cheese mixture, then the remaining half, until combined. Pour onto the prepared crust, smoothing the top with an offset spatula, and refrigerate for 6 hours.

**6.** To serve, lift entire dessert out of the pan using the overhanging parchment. Cut into sixteen 2-inch squares and serve with the strawberry sauce. If the cheesecake proves too soft to cut, freeze it for 30 minutes, then use a hot knife to cut. Refrigerate any remaining bars for up to 3 days.

# Old-Fashioned Strawberry Icebox Cake

**MAKES ONE 9- BY 13-INCH CAKE (12–14 SERVINGS)**

- 2 pounds fresh strawberries, hulled and sliced, plus more for garnish
- 2 tablespoons granulated sugar
- 3 cups heavy whipping cream
- ½ cup confectioners' sugar
- 1 teaspoon vanilla extract
- 15 chocolate graham cracker squares
- 30 graham cracker squares

*This traditional no-bake dessert is still popular today for family gatherings. The graham crackers soften to a cake-like consistency, making the cake easy to cut for serving.*

1. Toss the strawberries with the granulated sugar in a medium bowl.

2. Place the cream, confectioners' sugar, and vanilla in a large deep bowl. Using an electric hand mixer, whip until stiff peaks form, 3 to 4 minutes.

3. Spread a small amount of whipped cream on the bottom of a 9- by 13-inch baking dish. Place the chocolate graham crackers over the whipped cream. Cover with a third of the sliced strawberries. Spoon a layer of whipped cream (about a third of the volume) over the berries. Add a layer of 15 of the regular graham crackers topped with half of the remaining sliced strawberries, and top with half of the remaining whipped cream. Repeat for the final layer.

4. Cover the pan with plastic wrap or foil and refrigerate for at least 4 hours but no more than 12 hours. Cut into squares to serve, topped with a whole strawberry for garnish, if desired. Leftovers, although delicious, won't cut as cleanly the next day, so scoop them into a bowl for serving.

# English Summer Strawberry Trifle

**MAKES 8 SERVINGS**

- 1 (16-ounce) frozen store-bought pound cake, defrosted
- ¾ cups sugar
- ¼ cup cornstarch
- ¼ teaspoon salt
- 4 egg yolks, at room temperature
- 2 cups whole milk
- 2 teaspoons vanilla extract
- 1 cup heavy whipping cream
- ¼ cup cream sherry or simple syrup
- 1 pound fresh strawberries, hulled and sliced, reserving a few whole for garnish

*The English trifle, also known as a fool, is a traditional summer dish featuring the bounty of the berry season. Trifles are a classic example of using what is on hand, as early versions of the recipe were designed to use up leftover cake.*

1. Preheat the oven to 200°F (95°C).

2. Cut the pound cake into 1-inch cubes. Line a baking sheet with parchment paper and scatter with the pound cake cubes. Place the cubes in the oven to dry out while you prepare the remaining trifle ingredients.

3. Whisk together ½ cup of the sugar, the cornstarch, and salt in a large saucepan. Whisk in the egg yolks until smooth. Stir in ¼ cup of the milk and whisk until smooth. Stir in the remaining 1¾ cups milk. Heat the saucepan over medium heat, stirring constantly and scraping the bottom and sides of the pan with a silicone spatula, until the mixture thickens, about 10 minutes. Remove from the heat and stir in 1½ teaspoons of the vanilla. Cover the surface of the custard with a sheet of plastic wrap and let cool to room temperature.

4. Remove the pound cake cubes from the oven to cool.

5. Whip the cream, the remaining ¼ cup sugar, and the remaining ½ teaspoon vanilla in a large deep bowl using an electric hand mixer until stiff peaks form, 3 minutes.

6. When ready to assemble the trifle, divide one-third of the pound cake cubes evenly between 8 serving glasses. Drizzle with one-third of the sherry. Spoon one-third of the custard evenly over the pound cake. Dot with one-third of the strawberries. Spoon one-third of the whipped cream over the strawberries. Repeat twice with the remaining ingredients. Top with the reserved whole strawberries. Refrigerate for 1 hour before serving. Trifle is best served the same day. Leftovers may be covered with plastic wrap and eaten within 3 days. Although delicious, leftover trifle will be slightly soggy, and the pound cake cubes soften completely.

# Skillet Strawberry–Chocolate Chip Cookie

**MAKES ONE 10-INCH COOKIE (6–8 SERVINGS)**

- 1 cup (2 sticks) unsalted butter, at room temperature, plus more for the skillet
- ½ cup firmly packed light or dark brown sugar
- ½ cup granulated sugar
- 1 egg
- 1½ teaspoons vanilla extract
- 2½ cups all-purpose flour
- 1 teaspoon baking soda
- ½ teaspoon salt
- 1 cup semisweet chocolate chips
- ½ cup fresh strawberries, hulled and sliced
- Ice cream for serving (optional)

*A single skillet cookie is a fitting end to a family meal, served warm at the table with a scoop of ice cream. The strawberries add great color and a splash of fruity taste to this classic.*

1. Preheat the oven to 350°F (180°C). Grease a 10-inch skillet with butter and set aside.

2. Beat the butter and the sugars together in a large deep bowl using an electric hand mixer until well mixed, about 2 minutes. Stir in the egg and vanilla, and beat for 30 seconds.

3. Whisk together the flour, baking soda, and salt in a medium bowl until thoroughly combined, at least 30 seconds. Add it to the butter mixture, stirring well to mix. Fold ¾ cup of the chocolate chips into the batter. Spread the batter evenly in the skillet and sprinkle with the remaining ¼ cup chocolate chips. Top with the sliced strawberries, pressing them lightly into the top of the batter.

4. Bake for about 35 minutes, until golden brown. Cool for at least 30 minutes before cutting. If serving hot from the oven, the cookie won't slice, but it can be scooped into bowls and served with ice cream, if desired.

# Strawberry Thumbprint Cookies

**MAKES 20–25 COOKIES**

½ cup (1 stick) unsalted butter

1 egg, separated

¼ cup firmly packed light or dark brown sugar

¼ teaspoon ground nutmeg

½ teaspoon salt

1 cup all-purpose flour

1 teaspoon water

½ cup finely chopped pecans

Strawberry Jam (page 16 or 18)

*Thumbprint cookies of every stripe beg to be baked with a youngster at the baker's side. Make these cookies with any jam you have on hand.*

1. Preheat the oven to 300°F (150°C). Line a baking sheet with parchment paper.

2. Beat the butter, egg yolk, sugar, nutmeg, and salt in a deep bowl with an electric hand mixer until thoroughly combined, about 2 minutes. Stir in the flour. Dampen your hands and roll the dough into 20 to 25 small balls.

3. Lightly whisk the egg white with the water in a small bowl. Using one hand for dipping and one hand for rolling, dip each ball into the egg white mixture, then roll it in the chopped nuts. Place on the prepared baking sheet.

4. Bake the cookies for 5 minutes. Remove the pan from the oven and press a small well into each cookie using the back of a small spoon, such a half-teaspoon measure, or your thumb. Return the pan to the oven and bake for 15 minutes longer. Once you remove the cookies from the oven, spoon strawberry jam into each depression. Transfer the cookies to a wire rack to cool completely. These cookies freeze, well wrapped, for up to 3 months.

# ACKNOWLEDGMENTS

Single-subject books are my passion! I love a deep-dive into a single ingredient or cooking method. I am grateful to my acquisitions editor, Deanna Cook, who chose me to kick off this new fruit series for Storey Publishing. My editor, Sarah Guare, has corrected all my mistakes so that I look so much smarter than I am, and I remain indebted.

My agent, Lisa Ekus, introduced me to Deanna, and I'm so very glad. Thank you, Lisa, for being my biggest cheerleader.

A career as a cookbook author is incredibly rewarding. I love making connections with my readers and helping to solve their recipe challenges. If it were not for Nathalie Dupree, I would never have known I could have a career in food. Thank you for opening up my world.

My husband, Cliff, provides me with a lifestyle that allows me to write for pleasure. He is my champion, promoter, defender, and advocate. I am grateful to you, sweetie, and I am happy to still be in love these 33 years later. My adult children have become accomplished cooks in their own right. I'm so proud of them and all of their achievements.

To the farmers who till the soil, tend the fields, and produce my beloved berry, you are the rock stars I admire. Thank you for bringing such bounty to my table.

# INDEX